D1648168

Thoughts and Aphorisms

SRI AUROBINDO

Thoughts and Aphorisms

Sri Aurobindo Ashram
Pondicherry

First edition 1958
Sixth edition 2000
Fourth impression 2013

Rs 40
ISBN 978-81-7058-108-6

Published by Sri Aurobindo Ashram Publication Department
Pondicherry 605 002
Web http://www.sabda.in

Printed at Sri Aurobindo Ashram Press, Pondicherry
PRINTED IN INDIA

Publisher's Note

Thoughts and Aphorisms was written around 1913. Ten aphorisms from the manuscript were published in the monthly review *Arya* in 1915 and 1916 as parts of what was later issued as *Thoughts and Glimpses*. But the bulk of the aphorisms — that is, those included in the Karma, Jnana and Bhakti sections of the present booklet — were never published during Sri Aurobindo's lifetime. They first appeared in book form in 1958.

The seven "Additional Aphorisms" were first included in the edition of 1977; the last five were written in a separate manuscript notebook, apparently somewhat later than the others.

Jnana

Jnana

1.   There are two allied powers in man; knowledge & wisdom. Knowledge is so much of the truth seen in a distorted medium as the mind arrives at by groping, wisdom what the eye of divine vision sees in the spirit.

2.   Inspiration is a slender river of brightness leaping from a vast & eternal knowledge, it exceeds reason more perfectly than reason exceeds the knowledge of the senses.

3.   When I speak, the reason says, "This will I say"; but God takes the word out of my mouth and the lips say something else at which reason trembles.

4.   I am not a Jnani, for I have no knowledge except what God gives me for His work. How am I to know whether what I see be reason or folly? Nay, it is neither; for the thing seen is simply true & neither folly nor reason.

5.   If mankind could but see though in a glimpse of fleeting experience what infinite enjoyments, what perfect forces, what luminous reaches of spontaneous knowledge, what wide calms of our being lie waiting for us in the tracts which our animal evolution has not yet conquered, they would leave all & never rest till they had gained these treasures. But the way is narrow, the doors are hard to force, and fear, distrust & scepticism are there, sentinels of

Nature, to forbid the turning away of our feet from her ordinary pastures.

6.   Late, I learned that when reason died, then Wisdom was born; before that liberation, I had only knowledge.

7.   What men call knowledge, is the reasoned acceptance of false appearances. Wisdom looks behind the veil and sees.

8.   Reason divides, fixes details & contrasts them; Wisdom unifies, marries contrasts in a single harmony.

9.   Either do not give the name of knowledge to your beliefs only and of error, ignorance or charlatanism to the beliefs of others, or do not rail at the dogmas of the sects and their intolerance.

10.   What the soul sees and has experienced, that it knows; the rest is appearance, prejudice and opinion.

11.   My soul knows that it is immortal. But you take a dead body to pieces and cry triumphantly "Where is your soul and where is your immortality?"

12.   Immortality is not the survival of the mental personality after death, though that also is true, but the waking possession of the unborn & deathless self of which body is only an instrument and a shadow.

13.   They proved to me by convincing reasons that God did not exist, and I believed them. Afterwards I saw God,

for He came and embraced me. And now which am I to believe, the reasonings of others or my own experience?

14.　　They told me, "These things are hallucinations." I inquired what was a hallucination and found that it meant a subjective or a psychical experience which corresponds to no objective or no physical reality. Then I sat and wondered at the miracles of the human reason.

15.　　Hallucination is the term of Science for those irregular glimpses we still have of truths shut out from us by our preoccupation with matter; coincidence for the curious touches of artistry in the work of that supreme & universal Intelligence which in its conscious being as on a canvas has planned & executed the world.

16.　　That which men term a hallucination is the reflection in the mind & senses of that which is beyond our ordinary mental & sensory perceptions. Superstition arises from the mind's wrong understanding of these reflections. There is no other hallucination.

17.　　Do not, like so many modern disputants, smother thought under polysyllables or charm inquiry to sleep by the spell of formulas and cant words. Search always; find out the reason for things which seem to the hasty glance to be mere chance or illusion.

18.　　Someone was laying it down that God must be this or that or He would not be God. But it seemed to me that I can only know what God is and I do not see how I can tell Him what He ought to be. For what is the standard by which we can judge Him? These judgments are the follies of our egoism.

19.   Chance is not in this universe; the idea of illusion is itself an illusion. There was never illusion yet in the human mind that was not the concealing [?shape] and disfigurement of a truth.

20.   When I had the dividing reason, I shrank from many things; after I had lost it in sight, I hunted through the world for the ugly and the repellent, but I could no longer find them.

21.   God had opened my eyes; for I saw the nobility of the vulgar, the attractiveness of the repellent, the perfection of the maimed and the beauty of the hideous.

22.   Forgiveness is praised by the Christian and the Vaishnava, but for me, I ask, "What have I to forgive and whom?"

23.   God struck me with a human hand; shall I say then, "I pardon Thee thy insolence, O God"?

24.   God gave me good in a blow. Shall I say, "I forgive thee, O Almighty One, the harm and the cruelty, but do it not again"?

25.   When I pine at misfortune and call it evil, or am jealous and disappointed, then I know that there is awake in me again the eternal fool.

26.   When I see others suffer, I feel that I am unfortunate, but the wisdom that is not mine, sees the good that is coming and approves.

27.   Sir Philip Sidney said of the criminal led out to be hanged, "There, but for the grace of God, goes Sir Philip Sidney." Wiser, had he said, "There, by the grace of God, goes Sir Philip Sidney."

28.   God is a great & cruel Torturer because He loves. You do not understand this, because you have not seen & played with Krishna.

29.   One called Napoleon a tyrant and imperial cut-throat; but I saw God armed striding through Europe.

30.   I have forgotten what vice is and what virtue; I can only see God, His play in the world and His will in humanity.

31.   I saw a child wallowing in the dirt and the same child cleaned by his mother and resplendent, but each time I trembled before his utter purity.

32.   What I wished or thought to be the right thing, does not come about; therefore it is clear that there is no All Wise one who guides the world but only blind Chance or a brute Causality.

33.   The Atheist is God playing at hide & seek with Himself; but is the Theist any other? Well, perhaps; for he has seen the shadow of God and clutched at it.

34.   O Thou that lovest, strike! If Thou strike me not now, I shall know that Thou lov'st me not.

35.   O Misfortune, blessed be thou; for through thee I have seen the face of my Lover.

36.   Men are still in love with grief; when they see one who is too high for grief or joy, they curse him & cry, "O thou insensible!" Therefore Christ still hangs on the cross in Jerusalem.

37.   Men are in love with sin; when they see one who is too high for vice or virtue, they curse him & cry, "O thou breaker of bonds, thou wicked and immoral one!" Therefore Srikrishna does not live as yet in Brindavun.

38.   Some say Krishna never lived, he is a myth. They mean on earth; for if Brindavun existed nowhere, the Bhagwat could not have been written.

39.   Strange! the Germans have disproved the existence of Christ; yet his crucifixion remains still a greater historic fact than the death of Caesar.

40.   Sometimes one is led to think that only those things really matter which have never happened; for beside them most historic achievements seem almost pale and ineffective.

41.   There are four very great events in history, the siege of Troy, the life and crucifixion of Christ, the exile of Krishna in Brindavun and the colloquy with Arjuna on the

field of Kurukshetra. The siege of Troy created Hellas, the exile in Brindavun created devotional religion, (for before there was only meditation and worship,) Christ from his cross humanised Europe, the colloquy at Kurukshetra will yet liberate humanity. Yet it is said that none of these four events ever happened.

42.   They say that the Gospels are forgeries and Krishna a creation of the poets. Thank God then for the forgeries and bow down before the creators.

43.   If God assigns to me my place in Hell, I do not know why I should aspire to Heaven. He knows best what is for my welfare.

44.   If God draw me towards Heaven, then, even if His other hand strive to keep me in Hell, yet must I struggle upward.

45.   Only those thoughts are true the opposite of which is also true in its own time and application; indisputable dogmas are the most dangerous kind of falsehoods.

46.   Logic is the worst enemy of Truth, as self-righteousness is the worst enemy of virtue, — for the one cannot see its own errors nor the other its own imperfections.

47.   When I was asleep in the Ignorance, I came to a place of meditation full of holy men and I found their company wearisome and the place a prison; when I awoke, God took me to a prison and turned it into a place of meditation and His trysting-ground.

48.   When I read a wearisome book through and with pleasure, yet perceived all the perfection of its wearisomeness, then I knew that my mind was conquered.

49.   I knew my mind to be conquered when it admired the beauty of the hideous, yet felt perfectly why other men shrank back or hated.

50.   To feel & love the God of beauty and good in the ugly and the evil, and still yearn in utter love to heal it of its ugliness and its evil, this is real virtue and morality.

51.   To hate the sinner is the worst sin, for it is hating God; yet he who commits it, glories in his superior virtue.

52.   When I hear of a righteous wrath, I wonder at man's capacity for self-deception.

53.   This is a miracle that men can love God, yet fail to love humanity. With whom are they in love then?

54.   The quarrels of religious sects are like the disputing of pots, which shall be alone allowed to hold the immortalising nectar. Let them dispute, but the thing for us is to get at the nectar in whatever pot and attain immortality.

55.   You say that the flavour of the pot alters the liquor. That is taste; but what can deprive it of its immortalising faculty?

56.   Be wide in me, O Varuna; be mighty in me, O Indra; O Sun, be very bright and luminous; O Moon, be full

of charm and sweetness. Be fierce and terrible, O Rudra; be impetuous and swift, O Maruts; be strong and bold, O Aryama; be voluptuous and pleasurable, O Bhaga; be tender and kind and loving and passionate, O Mitra. Be bright and revealing, O Dawn; O Night, be solemn and pregnant. O Life, be full, ready & buoyant; O Death, lead my steps from mansion to mansion. Harmonise all these, O Brahmanaspati. Let me not be subject to these gods, O Kali.

57.   When, O eager disputant, thou hast prevailed in a debate, then art thou greatly to be pitied; for thou hast lost a chance of widening knowledge.

58.   Because the tiger acts according to his nature and knows not anything else, therefore he is divine and there is no evil in him. If he questioned himself, then he would be a criminal.

59.   The animal, before he is corrupted, has not yet eaten of the tree of the knowledge of good and evil; the god has abandoned it for the tree of eternal life; man stands between the upper heaven and the lower nature.

60.   One of the greatest comforts of religion is that you can get hold of God sometimes and give him a satisfactory beating. People mock at the folly of savages who beat their gods when their prayers are not answered; but it is the mockers who are the fools and the savages.

61.   There is no mortality. It is only the Immortal who can die; the mortal could neither be born nor perish. There

is nothing finite. It is only the Infinite who can make for Himself limits; the finite can have no beginning nor end, for the very act of conceiving its beginning & end declares its infinity.

62.   I heard a fool discoursing utter folly and wondered what God meant by it; then I considered and saw a distorted mask of truth and wisdom.

63.   God is great, says the Mahomedan. Yes, He is so great that He can afford to be weak, whenever that too is necessary.

64.   God often fails in His workings; it is the sign of His illimitable godhead.

65.   Because God is invincibly great, He can afford to be weak; because He is immutably pure, He can indulge with impunity in sin; He knows eternally all delight, therefore He tastes also the delight of pain; He is inalienably wise, therefore He has not debarred Himself from folly.

66.   Sin is that which was once in its place, persisting now it is out of place; there is no other sinfulness.

67.   There is no sin in man, but a great deal of disease, ignorance and misapplication.

68.   The sense of sin was necessary in order that man might become disgusted with his own imperfections. It was God's corrective for egoism. But man's egoism meets God's device by being very dully alive to its own sins and very keenly alive to the sins of others.

69.   Sin & virtue are a game of resistance we play with God in His efforts to draw us towards perfection. The sense of virtue helps us to cherish our sins in secret.

70.   Examine thyself without pity, then thou wilt be more charitable and pitiful to others.

71.   A thought is an arrow shot at the truth; it can hit a point, but not cover the whole target. But the archer is too well satisfied with his success to ask anything farther.

72.   The sign of dawning Knowledge is to feel that as yet I know little or nothing, & yet, if I could only know my knowledge, I already possess everything.

73.   When Wisdom comes, her first lesson is, "There is no such thing as knowledge; there are only aperçus of the Infinite Deity."

74.   Practical knowledge is a different thing; that is real and serviceable, but it is never complete. Therefore to systematise and codify it is necessary but fatal.

75.   Systematise we must, but even in making & holding the system, we should always keep firm hold on this truth that all systems are in their nature transitory and incomplete.

76.   Europe prides herself on her practical and scientific organisation and efficiency. I am waiting till her organisation is perfect; then a child shall destroy her.

77.   Genius discovers a system; average talent stereotypes it till it is shattered by fresh genius. It is dangerous for an army to be led by veterans; for on the other side God may place Napoleon.

78.   When knowledge is fresh in us, then it is invincible; when it is old, it loses its virtue. This is because God moves always forward.

79.   God is infinite Possibility. Therefore Truth is never at rest; therefore, also, Error is justified of her children.

80.   To listen to some devout people, one would imagine that God never laughs; Heine was nearer the mark when he found in Him the divine Aristophanes.

81.   God's laughter is sometimes very coarse and unfit for polite ears; He is not satisfied with being Molière, He must needs also be Aristophanes and Rabelais.

82.   If men took life less seriously, they could very soon make it more perfect. God never takes His works seriously; therefore one looks out on this wonderful Universe.

83.   Shame has admirable results and both in aesthetics and in morality we could ill spare it; but for all that it is a badge of weakness and the proof of ignorance.

84.   The supernatural is that the nature of which we have not attained or do not yet know, or the means of which we have not yet conquered. The common taste for miracles is the sign that man's ascent is not yet finished.

85.   It is rationality and prudence to distrust the supernatural; but to believe in it, is also a sort of wisdom.

86.   Great saints have performed miracles; greater saints
have railed at them; the greatest have both railed at them
and performed them.

87.   Open thy eyes and see what the world really is and
what God; have done with vain and pleasant imaginations.

88.   This world was built by Death that he might live.
Wilt thou abolish death? Then life too will perish. Thou
canst not abolish death, but thou mayst transform it into a
greater living.

89.   This world was built by Cruelty that she might love.
Wilt thou abolish cruelty? Then love too will perish. Thou
canst not abolish cruelty, but thou mayst transfigure it into
its opposite, into a fierce Love & Delightfulness.

90.   This world was built by Ignorance & Error that they
might know. Wilt thou abolish ignorance and error? Then
knowledge too will perish. Thou canst not abolish ignorance & error, but thou mayst transmute them into the
utter & effulgent exceeding of reason.

91.   If Life alone were & not death, there could be no
immortality; if love were alone & not cruelty, joy would be
only a tepid & ephemeral rapture; if reason were alone &
not ignorance, our highest attainment would not exceed a
limited rationality & worldly wisdom.

92.   Death transformed becomes Life that is Immortality; Cruelty transfigured becomes Love that is intolerable ecstasy; Ignorance transmuted becomes Light that leaps beyond wisdom and knowledge.

93.   Pain is the touch of our Mother teaching us how to bear and grow in rapture. She has three stages of her schooling, endurance first, next equality of soul, last ecstasy.

94.   All renunciation is for a greater joy yet ungrasped. Some renounce for the joy of duty done, some for the joy of peace, some for the joy of God and some for the joy of self-torture, but renounce rather as a passage to the freedom and untroubled rapture beyond.

95.   Only by perfect renunciation of desire or by perfect satisfaction of desire can the utter embrace of God be experienced; for in both ways the essential precondition is effected, — desire perishes.

96.   Experience in thy soul the truth of the Scripture; afterwards, if thou wilt, reason & state thy experience intellectually & even then distrust thy statement; but distrust never thy experience.

97.   When thou affirmest thy soul-experience & deniest the different soul-experience of another, know that God is making a fool of thee. Dost thou not hear His self-delighted laughter behind thy soul's curtains?

98.   Revelation is the direct sight, the direct hearing or the inspired memory of Truth, drishti, sruti, smriti; it is

the highest experience and always accessible to renewed experience. Not because God spoke it, but because the soul saw it, is the word of the Scriptures our supreme authority.

99.　The word of Scripture is infallible; it is in the interpretation the heart and reason put upon the Scripture that error has her portion.

100.　Shun all lowness, narrowness & shallowness in religious thought & experience. Be wider than the widest horizons, be loftier than the highest Kanchenjunga, be profounder than the deepest oceans.

101.　In God's sight there is no near or distant, no present, past or future. These things are only a convenient perspective for His world-picture.

102.　To the senses it is always true that the sun moves round the earth; this is false to the reason. To the reason it is always true that the earth moves round the sun; this is false to the supreme vision. Neither earth moves nor sun; there is only a change in the relation of sun-consciousness & earth-consciousness.

103.　Vivekananda, exalting Sannyasa, has said that in all Indian history there is only one Janaka. Not so, for Janaka is not the name of a single individual, but a dynasty of self-ruling kings and the triumph-cry of an ideal.

104.　In all the lakhs of ochre-clad Sannyasins, how many are perfect? It is the few attainments and the many approximations that justify an ideal.

105.   There have been hundreds of perfect Sannyasins, because Sannyasa had been widely preached and numerously practised; let it be the same with the ideal freedom and we shall have hundreds of Janakas.

106.   Sannyasa has a formal garb and outer tokens; therefore men think they can easily recognise it; but the freedom of a Janaka does not proclaim itself and it wears the garb of the world; to its presence even Narada was blinded.

107.   Hard is it to be in the world, free, yet living the life of ordinary men; but because it is hard, therefore it must be attempted and accomplished.

108.   When he watched the actions of Janaka, even Narada the divine sage thought him a luxurious worldling and libertine. Unless thou canst see the soul, how shalt thou say that a man is free or bound?

109.   All things seem hard to man that are above his attained level, & they are hard to his unaided effort; but they become at once easy & simple when God in man takes up the contract.

110.   To see the composition of the sun or the lines of Mars is doubtless a great achievement; but when thou hast the instrument that can show thee a man's soul as thou seest a picture, then thou wilt smile at the wonders of physical Science as the playthings of babies.

111.   Knowledge is a child with its achievements; for when it has found out something, it runs about the streets

whooping and shouting; Wisdom conceals hers for a long time in a thoughtful and mighty silence.

112. Science talks and behaves as if it had conquered all knowledge: Wisdom, as she walks, hears her solitary tread echoing on the margin of immeasurable Oceans.

113. Hatred is the sign of a secret attraction that is eager to flee from itself and furious to deny its own existence. That too is God's play in His creature.

114. Selfishness is the only sin, meanness the only vice, hatred the only criminality. All else can easily be turned into good, but these are obstinate resisters of deity.

115. The world is a long recurring decimal with Brahman for its integer. The period seems to begin and end, but the fraction is eternal; it will never have an end and never had any real beginning.

116. The beginning and end of things is a conventional term of our experience; in their true existence these terms have no reality, there is no end and no beginning.

117. "Neither is it that I was not before nor thou nor these kings nor that all we shall not be hereafter." Not only Brahman, but beings & things in Brahman are eternal; their creation and destruction is a play of hide and seek with our outward consciousness.

118. The love of solitude is a sign of the disposition towards knowledge; but knowledge itself is only achieved

when we have a settled perception of solitude in the crowd, in the battle and in the mart.

119.   If when thou art doing great actions and moving giant results, thou canst perceive that *thou* art doing nothing, then know that God has removed His seal from thy eyelids.

120.   If when thou sittest alone, still & voiceless on the mountaintop, thou canst perceive the revolutions thou art conducting, then hast thou the divine vision and art freed from appearances.

121.   The love of inaction is folly and the scorn of inaction is folly; there is no inaction. The stone lying inert upon the sands which is kicked away in an idle moment, has been producing its effect upon the hemispheres.

122.   If thou wouldst not be the fool of Opinion, first see wherein thy thought is true, then study wherein its opposite and contradiction is true; last, discover the cause of these differences and the key of God's harmony.

123.   An opinion is neither true nor false, but only serviceable for life or unserviceable; for it is a creation of Time and with time it loses its effect and value. Rise thou above opinion and seek wisdom everlasting.

124.   Use opinion for life, but let her not bind thy soul in her fetters.

125.   Every law, however embracing or tyrannous, meets somewhere a contrary law by which its operation can be checked, modified, annulled or eluded.

126. The most binding Law of Nature is only a fixed process which the Lord of Nature has framed and uses constantly; the Spirit made it and the Spirit can exceed it, but we must first open the doors of our prison-house and learn to live less in Nature than in the Spirit.

127. Law is a process or a formula; but the soul is the user of processes and exceeds formulas.

128. Live according to Nature, runs the maxim of the West; but according to what nature, the nature of the body or the nature which exceeds the body? This first we ought to determine.

129. O son of Immortality, live not thou according to Nature, but according to God; and compel her also to live according to the deity within thee.

130. Fate is God's foreknowledge outside Space & Time of all that in Space & Time shall yet happen; what He has foreseen, Power & Necessity work out by the conflict of forces.

131. Because God has willed and foreseen everything, thou shouldst not therefore sit inactive and wait upon His providence, for thy action is one of His chief effective forces. Up then and be doing, not with egoism, but as the circumstance, instrument and apparent cause of the event that He has predetermined.

132. When I knew nothing, then I abhorred the criminal, sinful and impure, being myself full of crime, sin and impurity; but when I was cleansed and my eyes unsealed, then I

bowed down in my spirit before the thief and the murderer
and adored the feet of the harlot; for I saw that these souls
had accepted the terrible burden of evil and drained for
all of us the greater portion of the churned poison of the
world-ocean.

133.   The Titans are stronger than the gods because they
have agreed with God to front and bear the burden of His
wrath and enmity; the gods were able to accept only the
pleasant burden of His love and kindlier rapture.

134.   When thou art able to see how necessary is suffering
to final delight, failure to utter effectiveness and retardation
to the last rapidity, then thou mayst begin to understand
something, however faintly and dimly, of God's workings.

135.   All disease is a means towards some new joy of
health, all evil & pain a tuning of Nature for some more
intense bliss & good, all death an opening on widest immortality. Why and how this should be so, is God's secret
which only the soul purified of egoism can penetrate.

136.   Why is thy mind or thy body in pain? Because thy
soul behind the veil wishes for the pain or takes delight in it;
but if thou wilt — and perseverest in thy will — thou canst
impose the spirit's law of unmixed delight on thy lower
members.

137.   There is no iron or ineffugable law that a given contact shall create pain or pleasure; it is the way the soul meets
the rush or pressure of Brahman upon the members from
outside them that determines either reaction.

138. The force of soul in thee meeting the same force from outside cannot harmonise the measures of the contact in values of mind-experience & body-experience, therefore thou hast pain, grief or uneasiness. If thou canst learn to adjust the replies of the force in thyself to the questions of world-force, thou shalt find pain becoming pleasurable or turning into pure delightfulness. Right relation is the condition of blissfulness, ritam the key of ananda.

139. Who is the superman? He who can rise above this matter-regarding broken mental human unit and possess himself universalised and deified in a divine force, a divine love & joy and a divine knowledge.

140. If thou keepest this limited human ego & thinkest thyself the superman, thou art but the fool of thy own pride, the plaything of thy own force and the instrument of thy own illusions.

141. Nietzsche saw the superman as the lion-soul passing out of camel-hood, but the true heraldic device & token of the superman is the lion seated upon the camel which stands upon the cow of plenty. If thou canst not be the slave of all mankind, thou art not fit to be its master and if thou canst not make thy nature as Vasistha's cow of plenty with all mankind to draw its wish from her udders, what avails thy leonine supermanhood?

142. Be to the world as the lion in fearlessness and lordship, as the camel in patience and service, as the cow in quiet, forbearing & maternal beneficence. Raven on all the joys of God as a lion over its prey, but bring also

all humanity into that infinite field of luxurious ecstasy to wallow there and to pasture.

143.   If Art's service is but to imitate Nature, then burn all the picture galleries and let us have instead photographic studios. It is because Art reveals what Nature hides, that a small picture is worth more than all the jewels of the millionaires and the treasures of the princes.

144.   If you only imitate visible Nature, you will perpetrate either a corpse, a dead sketch or a monstrosity; Truth lives in that which goes behind & beyond the visible & sensible.

145.   O Poet, O Artist, if thou but holdest up the mirror to Nature, thinkest thou Nature will rejoice in thy work? Rather she will turn away her face. For what dost thou hold up to her there? Herself? No, but a lifeless outline & reflection, a shadowy mimicry. It is the secret soul of Nature thou hast to seize, thou hast to hunt eternally after the truth in the external symbol, and that no mirror will hold for thee, nor for her whom thou seekest.

146.   I find in Shakespeare a far greater & more consistent universalist than the Greeks. All his creations are universal types from Lancelot Gobbo & his dog up to Lear & Hamlet.

147.   The Greeks sought universality by omitting all finer individual touches; Shakespeare sought it more successfully by universalising the rarest individual details of character. That which Nature uses for concealing from us the Infinite, Shakespeare used for revealing the Ananta-guna in man to the eye of humanity.

148. Shakespeare, who invented the figure of holding up the mirror to Nature, was the one poet who never condescended to a copy, a photograph or a shadow. The reader who sees in Falstaff, Macbeth, Lear or Hamlet imitations of Nature, has either no inner eye of the soul or has been hypnotised by a formula.

149. Where in material Nature wilt thou find Falstaff, Macbeth or Lear? Shadows & hints of them she possesses but they themselves tower above her.

150. There are two for whom there is hope, the man who has felt God's touch & been drawn to it and the sceptical seeker & self-convinced atheist; but for the formularists of all the religions & the parrots of free thought, they are dead souls who follow a death that they call living.

151. A man came to a scientist and wished to be instructed; this instructor showed him the revelations of the microscope & telescope, but the man laughed and said, "These are obviously hallucinations inflicted on the eye by the glass which you use as a medium; I will not believe till you show these wonders to my naked seeing." Then the scientist proved to him by many collateral facts & experiments the reliability of his knowledge but the man laughed again & said, "What you term proofs, I term coincidences, the number of coincidences does not constitute proof; as for your experiments, they are obviously effected under abnormal conditions & constitute a sort of insanity of Nature." When confronted with the results of mathematics, he was angry & cried out, "This is obviously imposture, gibberish & superstition; will you try to make me believe that these absurd cabalistic figures have any real force & meaning?"

Then the scientist drove him out as a hopeless imbecile; for he did not recognise his own system of denials and his own method of negative reasoning. If we wish to refuse an impartial & openminded enquiry, we can always find the most respectable polysyllables to cover our refusal or impose tests & conditions which stultify the enquiry.

152.   When our minds are involved in matter, they think matter the only reality; when we draw back into immaterial consciousness, then we see matter a mask and feel existence in consciousness alone as having the touch of reality. Which then of these two is the truth? Nay, God knoweth; but he who has had both experiences, can easily tell which condition is the more fertile in knowledge, the mightier & more blissful.

153.   I believe immaterial consciousness to be truer than material consciousness? Because I know in the first what in the second is hidden from me & also can command what the mind knows in matter.

154.   Hell & Heaven exist only in the soul's consciousness. Ay, but so does the earth and its lands & seas & fields & deserts & mountains & rivers. All world is nothing but arrangement of the Soul's seeing.

155.   There is only one soul & one existence; therefore we all see one objectivity only; but there are many knots of mind & ego in the one soul-existence, therefore we all see the one Object in different lights & shadows.

156.   The idealist errs; it is not Mind which created the worlds, but that which created mind has created them.

Mind only mis-sees, because it sees partially & by details, what is created.

157.   Thus said Ramakrishna and thus said Vivekananda. Yes, but let me know also the truths which the Avatar cast not forth into speech and the prophet has omitted from his teachings. There will always be more in God than the thought of man has ever conceived or the tongue of man has ever uttered.

158.   What was Ramakrishna? God manifest in a human being; but behind there is God in His infinite impersonality and His universal Personality. And what was Vivekananda? A radiant glance from the eye of Shiva; but behind him is the divine gaze from which he came and Shiva himself and Brahma and Vishnu and OM all-exceeding.

159.   He who recognises not Krishna, the God in man, knows not God entirely; he who knows Krishna only, knows not even Krishna. Yet is the opposite truth also wholly true that if thou canst see all God in a little pale unsightly and scentless flower, then hast thou hold of His supreme reality.

160.   Shun the barren snare of an empty metaphysics and the dry dust of an unfertile intellectuality. Only that knowledge is worth having which can be made use of for a living delight and put out into temperament, action, creation and being.

161.   Become & live the knowledge thou hast; then is thy knowledge the living God within thee.

162.   Evolution is not finished; reason is not the last word nor the reasoning animal the supreme figure of Nature. As man emerged out of the animal, so out of man the superman emerges.

163.   The power to observe law rigidly is the basis of freedom; therefore in most disciplines the soul has to endure & fulfil the law in its lower members before it can rise to the perfect freedom of its divine being. Those disciplines which begin with freedom are only for the mighty ones who are naturally free or in former lives have founded their freedom.

164.   Those who are deficient in the free, full and intelligent observation of a self-imposed law, must be placed in subjection to the will of others. This is one principal cause of the subjection of nations. After their disturbing egoism has been trampled under the feet of a master, they are given or, if they have force in them, attain a fresh chance of deserving liberty by liberty.

165.   To observe the law we have imposed on ourselves rather than the law of others is what is meant by liberty in our unregenerate condition. Only in God & by the supremacy of the spirit can we enjoy a perfect freedom.

166.   The double law of sin & virtue is imposed on us because we have not that ideal life & knowledge within which guides the soul spontaneously & infallibly to its self-fulfilment. The law of sin & virtue ceases for us when the sun of God shines upon the soul in truth & love with its unveiled splendour. Moses is replaced by Christ, the Shastra by the Veda.

167. God within is leading us always aright even when we are in the bonds of the ignorance; but then, though the goal is sure, it is attained by circlings & deviations.

168. The Cross is in Yoga the symbol of the soul & nature in their strong & perfect union, but because of our fall into the impurities of ignorance it has become the symbol of suffering and purification.

169. Christ came into the world to purify, not to fulfil. He himself foreknew the failure of his mission and the necessity of his return with the sword of God into a world that had rejected him.

170. Mahomed's mission was necessary, else we might have ended by thinking, in the exaggeration of our efforts at self-purification, that earth was meant only for the monk and the city created as a vestibule for the desert.

171. When all is said, Love & Force together can save the world eventually, but not Love only or Force only. Therefore Christ had to look forward to a second advent and Mahomed's religion, where it is not stagnant, looks forward through the Imams to a Mahdi.

172. Law cannot save the world, therefore Moses' ordinances are dead for humanity & the Shastra of the Brahmins is corrupt & dying. Law released into Freedom is the liberator. Not the Pandit, but the Yogin; not monasticism, but the inner renunciation of desire and ignorance & egoism.

173. Even Vivekananda once in the stress of emotion

admitted the fallacy that a personal God would be too immoral to be suffered and it would be the duty of all good men to resist Him. But if an omnipotent supra-moral Will & Intelligence governs the world, it is surely impossible to resist Him; our resistance would only serve His ends & really be dictated by Him. Is it not better then, instead of condemning or denying, to study and understand Him?

174.   If we would understand God, we must renounce our egoistic & ignorant human standards or else ennoble and universalise them.

175.   Because a good man dies or fails & the evil live & triumph, is God therefore evil? I do not see the logic of the consequence. I must first be convinced that death & failure are evil; I sometimes think that when they come, they are our supreme momentary good. But we are the fools of our hearts & nerves & argue that what they do not like or desire, must of course be an evil!

176.   When I look back on my past life, I see that if I had not failed & suffered, I would have lost my life's supreme blessings; yet at the time of the suffering & failure, I was vexed with the sense of calamity. Because we cannot see anything but the one fact under our noses, therefore we indulge in all these snifflings and clamours. Be silent, ye foolish hearts! slay the ego, learn to see & feel vastly & universally.

177.   The perfect cosmic vision & cosmic sentiment is the cure of all error & suffering; but most men succeed only in enlarging the range of their ego.

178.   Men say & think "For my country!" "For human-ity!" "For the world!" but they really mean "For myself seen in my country!" "For myself seen in humanity!" "For myself imaged to my fancy as the world!" That may be an enlargement, but it is not liberation. To be at large & to be in a large prison are not one condition of freedom.

179.   Live for God in thy neighbour, God in thyself, God in thy country & the country of thy foeman, God in humanity, God in tree & stone & animal, God in the world & outside the world, then art thou on the straight path to liberation.

180.   There are lesser & larger eternities, for eternity is a term of the soul & can exist in Time as well as exceeding it. When the Scriptures say "śaśwatih samah", they mean for a long space & permanence of time or a hardly measurable aeon; only God Absolute has the absolute eternity. Yet when one goes within, one sees that all things are secretly eternal; there is no end, neither was there ever a beginning.

181.   When thou callest another a fool, as thou must, sometimes, yet do not forget that thou thyself hast been the supreme fool in humanity.

182.   God loves to play the fool in season; man does it in season & out of season. It is the only difference.

183.   In the Buddhists' view to have saved an ant from drowning is a greater work than to have founded an empire. There is a truth in the idea, but a truth that can easily be exaggerated.

184.   To exalt one virtue,—compassion even,—unduly

above all others is to cover up with one's hand the eyes of wisdom. God moves always towards a harmony.

185.   Pity may be reserved, so long as thy soul makes distinctions, for the suffering animals; but humanity deserves from thee something nobler; it asks for love, for understanding, for comradeship, for the help of the equal & brother.

186.   The contributions of evil to the good of the world & the harm sometimes done by the virtuous are distressing to the soul enamoured of good. Nevertheless be not distressed nor confounded, but study rather & calmly understand God's ways with humanity.

187.   In God's providence there is no evil, but only good or its preparation.

188.   Virtue & vice were made for thy soul's struggle & progress; but for results they belong to God, who fulfils himself beyond vice & virtue.

189.   Live within; be not shaken by outward happenings.

190.   Fling not thy alms abroad everywhere in an ostentation of charity; understand & love where thou helpest. Let thy soul grow within thee.

191.   Help the poor while the poor are with thee; but study also & strive that there may be no poor for thy assistance.

192.   The old Indian social ideal demanded of the priest

voluntary simplicity of life, purity, learning and the gra-
tuitous instruction of the community, of the prince, war,
government, protection of the weak & the giving up of his
life in the battlefield, of the merchant, trade, gain and the
return of his gains to the community by free giving, of the
serf, labour for the rest & material havings. In atonement
for his serfhood, it spared him the tax of self-denial, the tax
of blood & the tax of his riches.

193.   The existence of poverty is the proof of an unjust &
ill-organised society, and our public charities are but the
first tardy awakening in the conscience of a robber.

194.   Valmekie, our ancient epic poet, includes among the
signs of a just & enlightened state of society not only universal education, morality and spirituality but this also that
there shall be "none who is compelled to eat coarse food,
none uncrowned & unanointed or who is restricted to a
mean and petty share of luxuries."

195.   The acceptance of poverty is noble & beneficial in a
class or an individual, but it becomes fatal and pauperises
life of its richness & expansion if it is perverted into a
general or national ideal. Athens, not Sparta, is the progressive type for mankind. Ancient India with its ideal of
vast riches & vast spending was the greatest of nations;
modern India with its trend towards national asceticism
has finally become poor in life & sunk into weakness &
degradation.

196.   Poverty is no more a necessity of organised social
life than disease of the natural body; false habits of life &

an ignorance of our true organisation are in both cases the peccant causes of an avoidable disorder.

197.   Do not dream that when thou hast got rid of material poverty, men will even so be happy or satisfied or society freed from ills, troubles & problems. This is only the first & lowest necessity. While the soul within remains defectively organised, there will always be outward unrest, disorder & revolution.

198.   Disease will always return to the body if the soul is flawed; for the sins of the mind are the secret cause of the sins of the body. So too poverty & trouble will always return on man in society, so long as the mind of the race is subjected to egoism.

199.   Religion & philosophy seek to rescue man from his ego; then the kingdom of heaven within will be spontaneously reflected in an external divine city.

200.   Mediaeval Christianity said to the race, "Man, thou art in thy earthly life an evil thing & a worm before God; renounce then egoism, live for a future state and submit thyself to God & His priest." The results were not over-good for humanity. Modern knowledge says to the race, "Man, thou art an ephemeral animal and no more to Nature than the ant & the earthworm, — a transitory speck only in the universe. Live then for the State & submit thyself antlike to the trained administrator & the scientific expert." Will this gospel succeed any better than the other?

201.   Vedanta says rather, "Man, thou art of one nature & substance with God, one soul with thy fellow-men. Awake

& progress then to thy utter divinity, live for God in thyself & in others." This gospel which was given only to the few, must now be offered to all mankind for its deliverance.

202. The human race always progresses most when most it asserts its importance to Nature, its freedom & its universality.

203. Animal man is the obscure starting-point, the present natural man the varied & tangled mid-road but supernatural man the luminous & transcendent goal of our human journey.

204. Life and action culminate and are eternally crowned for thee when thou hast attained the power of symbolising & manifesting in every thought & act, in wealth getting, wealth having or wealth spending, in home & government & society, in art, literature and life, the One Immortal in this lower mortal being.

Karma

Karma

205. God leads man while man is misleading himself, the higher nature watches over the stumblings of his lower mortality; this is the tangle & contradiction out of which we have to escape into the [?self-unity] to which alone is possible a clear knowledge & a faultless action.

206. That thou shouldst have pity on creatures, is well, but not well, if thou art a slave to thy pity. Be a slave to nothing except to God, not even to His most luminous angels.

207. Beatitude is God's aim for humanity; get this supreme good for thyself first that thou mayst distribute it entirely to thy fellow-beings.

208. He who acquires for himself alone, acquires ill though he may call it heaven and virtue.

209. In my ignorance I thought anger could be noble and vengeance grandiose; but now when I watch Achilles in his epic fury, I see a very fine baby in a very fine rage and I am pleased and amused.

210. Power is noble, when it overtops anger; destruction is grandiose, but it loses caste when it proceeds from vengeance. Leave these things, for they belong to a lower humanity.

211.   Poets make much of death and external afflictions; but the only tragedies are the soul's failures and the only epic man's triumphant ascent towards godhead.

212.   The tragedies of the heart & the body are the weeping of children over their little griefs & their broken toys. Smile within thyself, but comfort the children; join also, if thou canst, in their play.

213.   "There is always something abnormal and eccentric about men of genius." And why not? For genius itself is an abnormal birth and out of man's ordinary centre.

214.   Genius is Nature's first attempt to liberate the imprisoned god out of her human mould; the mould has to suffer in the process. It is astonishing that the cracks are so few and unimportant.

215.   Nature sometimes gets into a fury with her own resistance, then she damages the brain in order to free the inspiration; for in this effort the equilibrium of the average material brain is her chief opponent. Pass over the madness of such and profit by their inspiration.

216.   Who can bear Kali rushing into the system in her fierce force and burning godhead? Only the man whom Krishna already possesses.

217.   Hate not the oppressor, for, if he is strong, thy hate increases his force of resistance; if he is weak, thy hate was needless.

218.   Hatred is a sword of power, but its edge is always

double. It is like the Kritya of the ancient magicians which, if baulked of its prey, returned in fury to devour its sender.

219.   Love God in thy opponent, even while thou strikest him; so shall neither have hell for his portion.

220.   Men talk of enemies, but where are they? I only see wrestlers of one party or the other in the great arena of the universe.

221.   The saint and the angel are not the only divinities; admire also the Titan and the giant.

222.   The old writings call the Titans the elder gods. So they still are; nor is any god entirely divine unless there is hidden in him also a Titan.

223.   If I cannot be Rama, then I would be Ravana; for he is the dark side of Vishnu.

224.   Sacrifice, sacrifice, sacrifice always, but for the sake of God and humanity, not for the sake of sacrifice.

225.   Selfishness kills the soul; destroy it. But take care that your altruism does not kill the souls of others.

226.   Very usually, altruism is only the sublimest form of selfishness.

227.   He who will not slay when God bids him, works in the world an incalculable havoc.

228. Respect human life as long as you can; but respect more the life of humanity.

229. Men slay out of uncontrollable anger, hatred or vengeance; they shall suffer the rebound now or hereafter; or they slay to serve a selfish end, coldly; God shall not pardon them. If thou slay, first let thy soul have known death for a reality & seen God in the smitten, the stroke & the striker.

230. Courage and love are the only indispensable virtues; even if all the others are eclipsed or fall asleep, these two will save the soul alive.

231. Meanness & selfishness are the only sins that I find it difficult to pardon; yet they alone are almost universal. Therefore these also must not be hated in others, but in ourselves annihilated.

232. Nobleness and generosity are the soul's ethereal firmament; without them, one looks at an insect in a dungeon.

233. Let not thy virtues be such as men praise or reward, but such as make for thy perfection and God in thy nature demands of thee.

234. Altruism, duty, family, country, humanity are the prisons of the soul when they are not its instruments.

235. Our country is God the Mother; speak not evil of her unless thou canst do it with love and tenderness.

236.   Men are false to their country for their own profit; yet they go on thinking they have a right to turn in horror from the matricide.

237.   Break the moulds of the past, but keep safe its gains and its spirit, or else thou hast no future.

238.   Revolutions hew the past to pieces and cast it into a cauldron, but what has emerged is the old Aeson with a new visage.

239.   The world has had only half a dozen successful revolutions and most even of these were very like failures; yet it is by great & noble failures that humanity advances.

240.   Atheism is a necessary protest against the wickedness of the Churches and the narrowness of creeds. God uses it as a stone to smash these soiled card-houses.

241.   How much hatred & stupidity men succeed in packing up decorously and labelling "Religion"!

242.   God guides best when He tempts worst, loves entirely when He punishes cruelly, helps perfectly when violently He opposes.

243.   If God did not take upon Himself the burden of tempting men, the world would very soon go to perdition.

244.   Suffer yourself to be tempted within so that you may exhaust in the struggle your downward propensities.

245.   If you leave it to God to purify, He will exhaust the evil in you subjectively; but if you insist on guiding yourself, you will fall into much outward sin and suffering.

246.   Call not everything evil which men call evil, but only that reject which God has rejected; call not everything good which men call good, but accept only what God has accepted.

247.   Men in the world have two lights, duty and principle; but he who has passed over to God, has done with both and replaced them by God's will. If men abuse thee for this, care not, O divine instrument, but go on thy way like the wind or the sun fostering and destroying.

248.   Not to cull the praises of men has God made thee His own, but to do fearlessly His bidding.

249.   Accept the world as God's theatre; be thou the mask of the Actor and let Him act through thee. If men praise or hiss thee, know that they too are masks & take God within for thy only critic and audience.

250.   If Krishna be alone on one side and the armed & organised world with its hosts and its shrapnel and its Maxims on the other, yet prefer thy divine solitude. Care not if the world passes over thy body and its shrapnel tear thee to pieces and its cavalry trample thy limbs into shapeless mire by the wayside; for the mind was always a simulacrum and the body a carcass. The spirit liberated from its casings ranges and triumphs.

251.   If thou think defeat is the end of thee, then go not

forth to fight, even though thou be the stronger. For Fate is not purchased by any man nor is Power bound over to her possessors. But defeat is not the end, it is only a gate or a beginning.

252. I have failed, thou sayest. Say rather that God is circling about towards His object.

253. Foiled by the world, thou turnest to seize upon God. If the world is stronger than thou, thinkest thou God is weaker? Turn to Him rather for His bidding and for strength to fulfil it.

254. So long as a cause has on its side one soul that is intangible in faith, it cannot perish.

255. Reason gives me no basis for this faith, thou murmurest. Fool! if it did, faith would not be needed or demanded of thee.

256. Faith in the heart is the obscure & often distorted reflection of a hidden knowledge. The believer is often more plagued by doubt than the most inveterate sceptic. He persists because there is something subconscient in him which knows. That tolerates both his blind faith & twilit doubts and drives towards the revelation of that which it knows.

257. The world thinks that it moves by the light of reason but it is really impelled by its faiths and instincts.

258. Reason adapts itself to the faith or argues out a

justification of the instincts, but it receives the impulse subconsciously; therefore men think that they act rationally.

259.   The only business of reason is to arrange and criticise the perceptions. It has neither in itself any means of positive conclusion nor any command to action. When it pretends to originate or impel, it is masking other agencies.

260.   Until Wisdom comes to thee, use the reason for its God-given purposes and faith and instinct for theirs. Why shouldst thou set thy members to war upon each other?

261.   Perceive always and act in the light of thy increasing perceptions, but not those of the reasoning brain only. God speaks to the heart when the brain cannot understand him.

262.   If thy heart tell thee, Thus & by such means and at such a time it will happen, believe it not. But if it gives thee the purity and wideness of God's command, hearken to it.

263.   When thou hast the command, care only to fulfil it. The rest is God's will and arrangement which men call chance and luck and fortune.

264.   If thy aim be great and thy means small, still act; for by action alone these can increase to thee.

265.   Care not for time and success. Act out thy part, whether it be to fail or to prosper.

266.   There are three forms in which the command may come, the will and faith in thy nature, thy ideal on which

heart and brain are agreed and the voice of Himself or His angels.

267.   There are times when action is unwise or impossible; then go into tapasya in some physical solitude or in the retreats of thy soul and await whatever divine word or manifestation.

268.   Leap not too quickly at all voices, for there are lying spirits ready to deceive thee; but let thy heart be pure and afterwards listen.

269.   There are times when God seems to be sternly on the side of the past; then what has been and is, sits firm as on a throne and clothes itself with an irrevocable "I shall be". Then persevere, though thou seem to be fighting the Master of all; for this is His sharpest trial.

270.   All is not settled when a cause is humanly lost and hopeless; all is settled, only when the soul renounces its effort.

271.   He who would win high spiritual degrees, must pass endless tests and examinations. But most are anxious only to bribe the examiner.

272.   Fight, while thy hands are free, with thy hands and thy voice and thy brain and all manner of weapons. Art thou chained in the enemy's dungeons and have his gags silenced thee? Fight with thy silent all-besieging soul and thy wide-ranging will-power and when thou art dead, fight still with the world-encompassing force that went out from God within thee.

273.   Thou thinkest the ascetic in his cave or on his mountaintop a stone and a do-nothing? What dost thou know? He may be filling the world with the mighty currents of his will & changing it by the pressure of his soul-state.

274.   That which the liberated sees in his soul on its mountaintops, heroes and prophets spring up in the material world to proclaim and accomplish.

275.   The Theosophists are wrong in their circumstances but right in the essential. If the French Revolution took place, it was because a soul on the Indian snows dreamed of God as freedom, brotherhood and equality.

276.   All speech and action comes prepared out of the eternal Silence.

277.   There is no disturbance in the depths of the Ocean, but above there is the joyous thunder of its shouting and its racing shoreward; so is it with the liberated soul in the midst of violent action. The soul does not act; it only breathes out from itself overwhelming action.

278.   O soldier and hero of God, where for thee is sorrow or shame or suffering? For thy life is a glory, thy deeds a consecration, victory thy apotheosis, defeat thy triumph.

279.   Do thy lower members still suffer the shock of sin and sorrow? But above, seen of thee or unseen, thy soul sits royal, calm, free and triumphant. Believe that the Mother will ere the end have done her work and made the very earth of thy being a joy and a purity.

280.   If thy heart is troubled within thee, if for long seasons thou makest no progress, if thy strength faint and repine, remember always the eternal word of our Lover and Master, "I will free thee from all sin and evil; do not grieve."

281.   Purity is in thy soul; but for actions, where is their purity or impurity?

282.   O Death, our masked friend and maker of opportunities, when thou wouldst open the gate, hesitate not to tell us beforehand; for we are not of those who are shaken by its iron jarring.

283.   Death is sometimes a rude valet; but when he changes this robe of earth for that brighter raiment, his horseplay and impertinences can be pardoned.

284.   Who shall slay thee, O soul immortal? Who shall torture thee, O God ever-joyous?

285.   Think this when thy members would fain make love with depression and weakness, "I am Bacchus and Ares and Apollo; I am Agni pure and invincible; I am Surya ever burning mightily."

286.   Shrink not from the Dionysian cry & rapture within thee, but see that thou be not a straw upon those billows.

287.   Thou hast to learn to bear all the gods within thee and never stagger with their inrush or break under their burden.

288.   Mankind have wearied of strength and joy and called sorrow and weakness virtue, wearied of knowledge and called ignorance holiness, wearied of love and called heartlessness enlightenment and wisdom.

289.   There are many kinds of forbearance. I saw a coward hold out his cheek to the smiter; I saw a physical weakling struck by a strong and self-approving bully look quietly & intently at the aggressor; I saw God incarnate smile lovingly on those who stoned him. The first was ridiculous, the second terrible, the third divine and holy.

290.   It is noble to pardon thine own injurers, but not so noble to pardon wrongs done to others. Nevertheless pardon these too, but when needful, calmly avenge.

291.   When Asiatics massacre, it is an atrocity; when Europeans, it is a military exigency. Appreciate the distinction and ponder over this world's virtues.

292.   Watch the too indignantly righteous. Before long you will find them committing or condoning the very offence which they have so fiercely censured.

293.   "There is very little real hypocrisy among men." True, but there is a great deal of diplomacy and still more of self-deceit. The last is of three varieties, conscious, subconscious and half-conscious; but the third is the most dangerous.

294.   Be not deceived by men's shows of virtue, neither disgusted by their open or secret vices. These things are the necessary shufflings in a long transition-period of humanity.

295. Be not repelled by the world's crookednesses; the world is a wounded and venomous snake wriggling towards a destined off-sloughing and perfection. Wait; for it is a divine wager, and out of this baseness, God will emerge brilliant and triumphant.

296. Why dost thou recoil from a mask? Behind its odious, grotesque or terrible seemings Krishna laughs at thy foolish anger, thy more foolish scorn or loathing and thy most foolish terror.

297. When thou findest thyself scorning another, look then at thy own heart and laugh at thy folly.

298. Avoid vain disputing; but exchange views freely. If dispute thou must, learn from thy adversary; for even from a fool, if thou listen not with the ear and the reasoning mind but the soul's light, thou canst gather much wisdom.

299. Turn all things to honey; this is the law of divine living.

300. Private dispute should always be avoided; but shrink not from the public battle; yet even there appreciate the strength of thy adversary.

301. When thou hearest an opinion that displeases thee, study and find out the truth in it.

302. The mediaeval ascetics hated women and thought they were created by God for the temptation of monks. One may be allowed to think more nobly both of God and of woman.

303.   If a woman has tempted thee, is it her fault or thine? Be not a fool and a self-deceiver.

304.   There are two ways of avoiding the snare of woman; one is to shun all women and the other to love all beings.

305.   Asceticism is no doubt very healing, a cave very peaceful and the hill-tops wonderfully pleasant; nevertheless do thou act in the world as God intended thee.

306.   Three times God laughed at Shankara, first, when he returned to burn the corpse of his mother, again when he commented on the Isha Upanishad and the third time when he stormed about India preaching inaction.

307.   Men labour only after success and if they are fortunate enough to fail, it is because the wisdom and force of Nature overbear their intellectual cleverness. God alone knows when & how to blunder wisely and fail effectively.

308.   Distrust the man who has never failed and suffered; follow not his fortunes, fight not under his banner.

309.   There are two who are unfit for greatness and freedom, the man who has never been a slave to another and the nation that has never been under the yoke of foreigners.

310.   Fix not the time and the way in which the ideal shall be fulfilled. Work and leave time and way to God all-knowing.

311.   Work as if the ideal had to be fulfilled swiftly & in thy lifetime; persevere as if thou knewest it not to be unless

purchased by a thousand years yet of labour. That which thou darest not expect till the fifth millennium, may bloom out with tomorrow's dawning and that which thou hopest and lustest after now, may have been fixed for thee in thy hundredth advent.

312.   Each man of us has a million lives yet to fulfil upon earth. Why then this haste and clamour and impatience?

313.   Stride swiftly for the goal is far; rest not unduly, for thy Master is waiting for thee at the end of thy journey.

314.   I am weary of the childish impatience which cries & blasphemes and denies the ideal because the Golden Mountains cannot be reached in our little day or in a few momentary centuries.

315.   Fix thy soul without desire upon the end and insist on it by the divine force within thee; then shall the end itself create its means, nay, it shall become its own means. For the end is Brahman and already accomplished; see it always as Brahman, see it always in thy soul as already accomplished.

316.   Plan not with the intellect, but let thy divine sight arrange thy plans for thee. When a means comes to thee as thing to be done, make that thy aim; as for the end, it is, in world, accomplishing itself and, in thy soul, already accomplished.

317.   Men see events as unaccomplished, to be striven for and effected. This is false seeing; events are not effected, they develop. The event is Brahman, already accomplished from of old, it is now manifesting.

318. As the light of a star reaches the earth hundreds of years after the star has ceased to exist, so the event already accomplished in Brahman at the beginning manifests itself now in our material experience.

319. Governments, societies, kings, police, judges, institutions, churches, laws, customs, armies are temporary necessities imposed on us for a few groups of centuries because God has concealed His face from us. When it appears to us again in its truth & beauty, then in that light they will vanish.

320. The anarchic is the true divine state of man in the end as in the beginning; but in between it would lead us straight to the devil and his kingdom.

321. The communistic principle of society is intrinsically as superior to the individualistic as is brotherhood to jealousy and mutual slaughter; but all the practical schemes of Socialism invented in Europe are a yoke, a tyranny and a prison.

322. If communism ever reestablishes itself successfully upon earth, it must be on a foundation of soul's brotherhood and the death of egoism. A forced association and a mechanical comradeship would end in a worldwide fiasco.

323. Vedanta realised is the only practicable basis for a communistic society. It is the kingdom of the saints dreamed of by Christianity, Islam and Puranic Hinduism.

324. "Freedom, equality, brotherhood," cried the French revolutionists, but in truth freedom only has been practised

with a dose of equality; as for brotherhood, only a brotherhood of Cain was founded — and of Barabbas. Sometimes it calls itself a Trust or Combine and sometimes the Concert of Europe.

325. "Since liberty has failed," cries the advanced thought of Europe, "let us try liberty cum equality or, since the two are a little hard to pair, equality instead of liberty. For brotherhood, it is impossible; therefore we will replace it by industrial association." But this time also, I think, God will not be deceived.

326. India had three fortresses of a communal life, the village community, the larger joint family & the orders of the Sannyasins; all these are broken or breaking with the stride of egoistic conceptions of social life; but is not this after all only the breaking of these imperfect moulds on the way to a larger & diviner communism?

327. The individual cannot be perfect until he has surrendered all he now calls himself to the divine Being. So also, until mankind gives all it has to God, never shall there be a perfected society.

328. There is nothing small in God's eyes; let there be nothing small in thine. He bestows as much labour of divine energy on the formation of a shell as on the building of an empire. For thyself it is greater to be a good shoemaker than a luxurious and incompetent king.

329. Imperfect capacity & effect in the work that is meant for thee is better than an artificial competency & a borrowed perfection.

330.   Not result is the purpose of action, but God's eternal delight in becoming, seeing and doing.

331.   God's world advances step by step fulfilling the lesser unit before it seriously attempts the larger. Affirm free nationality first, if thou wouldst ever bring the world to be one nation.

332.   A nation is not made by a common blood, a common tongue or a common religion; these are only important helps and powerful conveniences. But wherever communities of men not bound by family ties are united in one sentiment and aspiration to defend a common inheritance from their ancestors or assure a common future for their posterity, there a nation is already in existence.

333.   Nationality is a stride of the progressive God passing beyond the stage of the family; therefore the attachment to clan and tribe must weaken or perish before a nation can be born.

334.   Family, nationality, humanity are Vishnu's three strides from an isolated to a collective unity. The first has been fulfilled, we yet strive for the perfection of the second, towards the third we are reaching out our hands and the pioneer work is already attempted.

335.   With the present morality of the human race a sound and durable human unity is not yet possible; but there is no reason why a temporary approximation to it should not be the reward of strenuous aspiration and untiring effort. By constant approximations and by partial realisations and temporary successes Nature advances.

336. Imitation is sometimes a good training-ship; but it will never fly the flag of the admiral.

337. Rather hang thyself than belong to the horde of successful imitators.

338. Tangled is the way of works in the world. When Rama the Avatar murdered Vali or Krishna, who was God himself, assassinated, to liberate his nation, his tyrant uncle Kansa, who shall say whether they did good or did evil? But this we can feel, that they acted divinely.

339. Reaction perfects & hastens progress by increasing & purifying the force within it. This is what the multitude of the weak cannot see who despair of their port when the ship is fleeing helplessly before the storm wind, but it flees, hidden by the rain & the Ocean furrow, towards God's intended haven.

340. Democracy was the protest of the human soul against the allied despotisms of autocrat, priest and noble; Socialism is the protest of the human soul against the despotism of a plutocratic democracy; Anarchism is likely to be the protest of the human soul against the tyranny of a bureaucratic Socialism. A turbulent and eager march from illusion to illusion and from failure to failure is the image of European progress.

341. Democracy in Europe is the rule of the Cabinet minister, the corrupt deputy or the self-seeking capitalist masqued by the occasional sovereignty of a wavering populace; Socialism in Europe is likely to be the rule of the

official and policeman masqued by the theoretic sovereignty of an abstract State. It is chimerical to enquire which is the better system; it would be difficult to decide which is the worse.

342.   The gain of democracy is the security of the individual's life, liberty and goods from the caprices of the tyrant one or the selfish few; its evil is the decline of greatness in humanity.

343.   This erring race of human beings dreams always of perfecting their environment by the machinery of government and society; but it is only by the perfection of the soul within that the outer environment can be perfected. What thou art within, that outside thee thou shalt enjoy; no machinery can rescue thee from the law of thy being.

344.   Be always vigilant against thy human proneness to persecute or ignore the reality even while thou art worshipping its semblance or token. Not human wickedness but human fallibility is the opportunity of Evil.

345.   Honour the garb of the ascetic, but look also at the wearer, lest hypocrisy occupy the holy places and inward saintliness become a legend.

346.   The many strive after competence or riches, the few embrace poverty as a bride; but, for thyself, strive after and embrace God only. Let Him choose for thee a king's palace or the bowl of the beggar.

347.   What is vice but an enslaving habit and virtue but a

human opinion? See God and do His will; walk in whatever path He shall trace for thy goings.

348. In the world's conflicts espouse not the party of the rich for their riches, nor of the poor for their poverty, of the king for his power & majesty, nor of the people for their hope and fervour, but be on God's side always. Unless indeed He has commanded thee to war against Him! then do that with thy whole heart and strength and rapture.

349. How shall I know God's will with me? I have to put egoism out of me, hunting it from every lair & burrow, and bathe my purified and naked soul in His infinite workings; then He himself will reveal it to me.

350. Only the soul that is naked and unashamed, can be pure and innocent, even as Adam was in the primal garden of humanity.

351. Boast not thy riches, neither seek men's praise for thy poverty and self-denial; both these things are the coarse or the fine food of egoism.

352. Altruism is good for man, but less good when it is a form of supreme self-indulgence & lives by pampering the selfishness of others.

353. By altruism thou canst save thy soul, but see that thou save it not by indulging in his perdition thy brother.

354. Self-denial is a mighty instrument for purification; it is not an end in itself nor a final law of living. Not to

mortify thyself but to satisfy God in the world must be thy object.

355.   It is easy to distinguish the evil worked by sin & vice, but the trained eye sees also the evil done by self-righteous or self-regarding virtue.

356.   The Brahmin first ruled by the book & the ritual, the Kshatriya next by the sword and the buckler; now the Vaishya governs us by machinery & the dollar, & the Sudra, the liberated serf, presses in with his doctrine of the kingdom of associated labour. But neither priest, king, merchant nor labourer is the true governor of humanity; the despotism of the tool and the mattock will fail like all the preceding despotisms. Only when egoism dies & God in man governs his own human universality, can this earth support a happy and contented race of beings.

357.   Men run after pleasure and clasp feverishly that burning bride to their tormented bosoms; meanwhile a divine & faultless bliss stands behind them waiting to be seen and claimed and captured.

358.   Men hunt after petty successes & trivial masteries from which they fall back into exhaustion & weakness; meanwhile all the infinite force of God in the universe waits vainly to place itself at their disposal.

359.   Men burrow after little details of knowledge and group them into bounded & ephemeral thought systems; meanwhile all infinite wisdom laughs above their heads & shakes wide the glory of her iridescent pinions.

360. Men seek laboriously to satisfy & complement the little bounded being made of the mental impressions they have grouped about a mean & grovelling ego; meanwhile the spaceless & timeless Soul is denied its joyous & splendid manifestation.

361. O soul of India, hide thyself no longer with the darkened Pandits of the Kaliyuga in the kitchen & the chapel, veil not thyself with the soulless rite, the obsolete law and the unblessed money of the dakshina; but seek in thy soul, ask of God and recover thy true Brahminhood & Kshatriyahood with the eternal Veda; restore the hidden truth of the Vedic sacrifice, return to the fulfilment of an older & mightier Vedanta.

362. Limit not sacrifice to the giving up of earthly goods or the denial of some desires & yearnings, but let every thought and every work & every enjoyment be an offering to God within thee. Let thy steps walk in thy Lord, let thy sleep and waking be a sacrifice to Krishna.

363. This is not according to my Shastra or my Science, say the men of rule, formalists. Fool! is God then only a book that there should be nothing true & good except what is written?

364. By which standard shall I walk, the word that God speaks to me, saying "This is My will, O my servant," or the rules that men who are dead, have written? Nay, if I have to fear & obey any, I will fear & obey God rather & not the pages of a book or the frown of a Pandit.

365. Thou mayst be deceived, wilt thou say, it may not be

God's voice leading thee? Yet do I know that He abandons not those who have trusted Him even ignorantly, yet have I found that He leads wisely & lovingly even when He seems to deceive utterly, yet would I rather fall into the snare of the living God than be saved by trust in a dead formulary.

366.   Act according to the Shastra rather than thy self-will & desire; so shalt thou grow stronger to control the ravener in thee; but act according to God rather than the Shastra; so shalt thou reach to His highest which is far above rule & limit.

367.   The Law is for the bound & those whose eyes are sealed; if they walk not by it, they will stumble; but thou who art free in Krishna or hast seen his living light, walk holding the hand of thy Friend & by the lamp of eternal Veda.

368.   The Vedanta is God's lamp to lead thee out of this night of bondage & egoism; but when the light of Veda has dawned in thy soul, then even that divine lamp thou needest not, for now thou canst walk freely & surely in a high & eternal sunlight.

369.   What is the use of only knowing? I say to thee, Act and be, for therefore God sent thee into this human body.

370.   What is the use of only being? I say to thee, Become, for therefore wast thou established as a man in this world of matter.

371.   The path of works is in a way the most difficult side of God's triune causeway; yet is it not also, in this material

world at least, the easiest, widest & most delightful? For at every moment we clash against God the worker & grow into His being by a thousand divine touches.

372. This is the wonder of the way of works that even enmity to God can be made an agency of salvation. Sometimes God draws and attaches us most swiftly to Him by wrestling with us as our fierce, invincible & irreconcilable enemy.

373. Shall I accept death or shall I turn and wrestle with him and conquer? That shall be as God in me chooses. For whether I live or die, I am always.

374. What is this thing thou callest death? Can God die? O thou who fearest death, it is Life that has come to thee sporting with a death-head and wearing a mask of terror.

375. There is a means to attain physical immortality and death is by our choice, not by Nature's compulsion. But who would care to wear one coat for a hundred years or be confined in one narrow & changeless lodging unto a long eternity?

376. Fear and anxiety are perverse forms of will. What thou fearest & ponderest over, striking that note repeatedly in thy mind, thou helpest to bring about; for, if thy will above the surface of waking repels it, it is yet what thy mind underneath is all along willing, & the subconscious mind is mightier, wider, better equipped to fulfil than thy waking force & intellect. But the spirit is stronger than both together; from fear and hope take refuge in the grandiose calm and careless mastery of the spirit.

377. God made the infinite world by Self-knowledge which in its works is Will-Force self-fulfilling. He used ignorance to limit His infinity; but fear, weariness, depression, self-distrust and assent to weakness are the instruments by which He destroys what He created. When these things are turned on what is evil or harmful & ill-regulated within thee, then it is well; but if they attack thy very sources of life & strength, then seize & expel them or thou diest.

378. Mankind has used two powerful weapons to destroy its own powers and enjoyment, wrong indulgence and wrong abstinence.

379. Our mistake has been and is always to flee from the ills of Paganism to asceticism as a remedy and from the ills of asceticism back to Paganism. We swing for ever between two false opposites.

380. It is well not to be too loosely playful in one's games or too grimly serious in one's life and works. We seek in both a playful freedom and a serious order.

381. For nearly forty years I believed them when they said I was weakly in constitution, suffered constantly from the smaller & the greater ailments & mistook this curse for a burden that Nature had laid upon me. When I renounced the aid of medicines, then they began to depart from me like disappointed parasites. Then only I understood what a mighty force was the natural health within me & how much mightier yet the Will & Faith exceeding mind which God meant to be the divine support of our life in this body.

382. Machinery is necessary to modern humanity because

of our incurable barbarism. If we must incase ourselves in a bewildering multitude of comforts and trappings, we must needs do without Art and its methods; for to dispense with simplicity & freedom is to dispense with beauty. The luxury of our ancestors was rich & even gorgeous, but never encumbered.

383. I cannot give to the barbarous comfort & encumbered ostentation of European life the name of civilisation. Men who are not free in their souls & nobly rhythmical in their appointments, are not civilised.

384. Art in modern times & under European influence has become an excrescence upon life or an unnecessary menial; it should have been its chief steward and indispensable arranger.

385. Disease is needlessly prolonged & ends in death oftener than is inevitable, because the mind of the patient supports & dwells upon the disease of his body.

386. Medical Science has been more a curse to mankind than a blessing. It has broken the force of epidemics and unveiled a marvellous surgery; but, also, it has weakened the natural health of man and multiplied individual diseases; it has implanted fear and dependence in the mind and body; it has taught our health to repose not on natural soundness but a rickety & distasteful crutch compact from the mineral and vegetable kingdoms.

387. The doctor aims a drug at a disease; sometimes it hits, sometimes misses. The misses are left out of account, the hits treasured up, reckoned and systematised into a science.

388.　We laugh at the savage for his faith in the medicine man; but how are the civilised less superstitious who have faith in the doctors? The savage finds that when a certain incantation is repeated, he often recovers from a certain disease; he believes. The civilised patient finds that when he doses himself according to a certain prescription, he often recovers from a certain disease; he believes. Where is the difference?

389.　The north-country Indian herdsman, attacked by fever, sits in the chill stream of a river for an hour or more & rises up free & healthy. If the educated man did the same, he would perish, not because the same remedy in its nature kills one & cures another, but because our bodies have been fatally indoctrinated by the mind into false habits.

390.　It is not the medicine that cures so much as the patient's faith in the doctor and the medicine. Both are a clumsy substitute for the natural faith in one's own self-power which they have themselves destroyed.

391.　The healthiest ages of mankind were those in which there were the fewest material remedies.

392.　The most robust and healthy race left on earth were the African savages; but how long can they so remain after their physical consciousness has been contaminated by the mental aberrations of the civilised?

393.　We ought to use the divine health in us to cure and prevent diseases; but Galen and Hippocrates & their tribe have given us instead an armoury of drugs and a barbarous Latin hocuspocus as our physical gospel.

394. Medical Science is well-meaning and its practitioners often benevolent and not seldom self-sacrificing; but when did the well-meaning of the ignorant save them from harm-doing?

395. If all remedies were really and in themselves efficacious and all medical theories sound, how would that console us for our lost natural health and vitality? The upas-tree is sound in all its parts, but it is still an upas-tree.

396. The spirit within us is the only all-efficient doctor and submission of the body to it the one true panacea.

397. God within is infinite and self-fulfilling Will. Unappalled by the fear of death, canst thou leave to Him, not as an experiment, with a calm & entire faith thy ailments? Thou shalt find in the end that He exceeds the skill of a million doctors.

398. Health protected by twenty thousand precautions is the gospel of the doctor; but it is not God's evangel for the body, nor Nature's.

399. Man was once naturally healthy and could revert to that primal condition if he were suffered; but Medical Science pursues our body with an innumerable pack of drugs and assails the imagination with ravening hordes of microbes.

400. I would rather die and have done with it than spend life in defending myself against a phantasmal siege of microbes. If that is to be barbarous [and] unenlightened, I embrace gladly my Cimmerian darkness.

401. Surgeons save & cure by cutting and maiming. Why not rather seek to discover Nature's direct all-powerful remedies?

402. It should take long for self-cure to replace medicine, because of the fear, self-distrust and unnatural physical reliance on drugs which Medical Science has taught to our minds & bodies & made our second nature.

403. Medicine is necessary for our bodies in disease only because our bodies have learned the art of not getting well without medicines. Even so, one sees often that the moment Nature chooses for recovery is that in which the life is abandoned as hopeless by the doctors.

404. Distrust of the curative power within us was our physical fall from Paradise. Medical Science and a bad heredity are the two angels of God who stand at the gates to forbid our return and reentry.

405. Medical Science to the human body is like a great Power which enfeebles a smaller State by its protection or like a benevolent robber who knocks his victim flat and riddles him with wounds in order that he may devote his life to healing & serving the shattered body.

406. Drugs often cure the body when they do not merely trouble or poison it, but only if their physical attack on the disease is supported by the force of the spirit; if that force can be made to work freely, drugs are at once superfluous.

Bhakti

Bhakti

407. I am not a Bhakta, for I have not renounced the world for God. How can I renounce what He took from me by force and gave back to me against my will? These things are too hard for me.

408. I am not a Bhakta, I am not a Jnani, I am not a worker for the Lord. What am I then? A tool in the hands of my Master, a flute blown upon by the divine Herd-Boy, a leaf driven by the breath of the Lord.

409. Devotion is not utterly fulfilled till it becomes action and knowledge. If thou pursuest after God and canst overtake Him, let Him not go till thou hast His reality. If thou hast hold of His reality, insist on having also His totality. The first will give thee divine knowledge, the second will give thee divine works and a free and perfect joy in the universe.

410. Others boast of their love for God. My boast is that I did not love God; it was He who loved me and sought me out and forced me to belong to Him.

411. After I knew that God was a woman, I learned something from far-off about love; but it was only when I became a woman and served my Master and Paramour that I knew love utterly.

412.   To commit adultery with God is the perfect experience for which the world was created.

413.   To fear God really is to remove oneself to a distance from Him, but to fear Him in play gives an edge to utter delightfulness.

414.   The Jew invented the God-fearing man; India the God-knower and God-lover.

415.   The servant of God was born in Judaea, but he came to maturity among the Arabs. India's joy is in the servant-lover.

416.   Perfect love casts out fear; but still keep thou some tender shadow and memory of the exile and it will make the perfection more perfect.

417.   Thy soul has not tasted God's entire delight, if it has never had the joy of being His enemy, opposing His designs and engaging with Him in mortal combat.

418.   If you cannot make God love you, make Him fight you. If He will not give you the embrace of the lover, compel Him to give you the embrace of the wrestler.

419.   My soul is the captive of God, taken by Him in battle; it still remembers the war, though so far from it, with delight and alarm and wonder.

420.   Most of all things on earth I hated pain till God hurt and tortured me; then it was revealed to me that pain is only a perverse and recalcitrant shape of excessive delight.

421. There are four stages in the pain God gives to us; when it is only pain; when it is pain that causes pleasure; when it is pain that is pleasure; and when it is purely a fiercer form of delight.

422. Even when one has climbed up into those levels of bliss where pain vanishes, it still survives disguised as intolerable ecstasy.

423. When I was mounting upon ever higher crests of His joy, I asked myself whether there was no limit to the increase of bliss and almost I grew afraid of God's embraces.

424. The next greatest rapture to the love of God, is the love of God in men; there, too, one has the joy of multiplicity.

425. For monogamy may be the best for the body, but the soul that loves God in men dwells here always as the boundless & ecstatic polygamist; yet all the time — that is the secret — it is in love with only one being.

426. The whole world is my seraglio and every living being and inanimate existence in it is the instrument of my rapture.

427. I did not know for some time whether I loved Krishna best or Kali; when I loved Kali, it was loving myself, but when I loved Krishna, I loved another, and still it was my Self with whom I was in love. Therefore I came to love Krishna better even than Kali.

428. What is the use of admiring Nature or worshipping

her as a Power, a Presence and a goddess? What is the use, either, of appreciating her aesthetically or artistically? The secret is to enjoy her with the soul as one enjoys a woman with the body.

429.   When one has the vision in the heart, everything, Nature and Thought and Action, ideas and occupations and tastes and objects become the Beloved and are a source of ecstasy.

430.   The philosophers who reject the world as Maya, are very wise and austere and holy; but I cannot help thinking sometimes that they are also just a little stupid and allow God to cheat them too easily.

431.   For my part, I think I have a right to insist on God giving Himself to me in the world as well as out of it. Why did He make it at all, if He wanted to escape that obligation?

432.   The Mayavadin talks of my Personal God as a dream and prefers to dream of Impersonal Being; the Buddhist puts that aside too as a fiction and prefers to dream of Nirvana and the bliss of nothingness. Thus all the dreamers are busy reviling each other's visions and parading their own as the panacea. What the soul utterly rejoices in, is for thought the ultimate reality.

433.   Beyond Personality the Mayavadin sees indefinable Existence; I followed him there and found my Krishna beyond in indefinable Personality.

434.   When I first met Krishna, I loved Him as a friend

and playmate till He deceived me; then I was indignant and could not forgive Him. Afterwards I loved Him as a lover and He still deceived me; I was again and much more indignant, but this time I had to pardon.

435.   After offending, He forced me to pardon Him not by reparation, but by committing fresh offences.

436.   So long as God tried to repair His offences against me, we went on periodically quarrelling; but when He found out His mistake, the quarrelling stopped, for I had to submit to Him entirely.

437.   When I saw others than Krishna and myself in the world, I kept secret God's doings with me; but since I began to see Him and myself everywhere, I have become shameless and garrulous.

438.   All that my Lover has, belongs to me. Why do you abuse me for showing off the ornaments He has given to me?

439.   My Lover took His crown and royal necklace from His head and neck and clothed me with them; but the disciples of the saints and the prophets abused me and said, "He is hunting after siddhis."

440.   I did my Lover's commands in the world & the will of my Captor; but they cried, "Who is this corruptor of youth, this disturber of morals?"

441.   If I cared even for your praise, O ye saints, if I cherished my reputation, O ye prophets, my Lover would never

have taken me into His bosom and given me the freedom of His secret chambers.

442.   I was intoxicated with the rapture of my Lover and I threw the robe of the world from me even in the world's highways. Why should I care that the worldlings mock and the Pharisees turn their faces?

443.   To thy lover, O Lord, the railing of the world is wild honey and the pelting of stones by the mob is summer rain on the body. For is it not Thou that railest and peltest, and is it not Thou in the stones that strikest and hurtest me?

444.   There are two things in God which men call evil, that which they cannot understand at all and that which they misunderstand and, possessing, misuse; it is only what they grope after half-vainly and dimly understand that they call good and holy. But to me all things in Him are lovable.

445.   They say, O my God, that I am mad because I see no fault in Thee; but if I am indeed mad with Thy love, I do not wish to recover my sanity.

446.   "Errors, falsehoods, stumblings!" they cry. How bright and beautiful are Thy errors, O Lord! Thy falsehoods save Truth alive; by Thy stumblings the world is perfected.

447.   Life, Life, Life, I hear the passions cry; God, God, God, is the soul's answer. Unless thou seest and lovest Life as God only, then is Life itself a sealed joy to thee.

448.   "He loves her", the senses say; but the soul says "God God God". That is the all-embracing formula of existence.

449.   If thou canst not love the vilest worm and the foulest of criminals, how canst thou believe that thou hast accepted God in thy spirit?

450.   To love God, excluding the world, is to give Him an intense but imperfect adoration.

451.   Is love only a daughter or handmaid of jealousy? If Krishna loves Chandrabali, why should I not love her also?

452.   Because thou lovest God only, thou art apt to claim that He should love thee rather than others; but this is a false claim contrary to right & the nature of things. For He is the One but thou art of the many. Rather become one in heart & soul with all beings, then there will be none in the world but thou alone for Him to love.

453.   My quarrel is with those who are foolish enough not to love my Lover, not with those who share His love with me.

454.   In those whom God loves, have delight; on those whom He pretends not to love, take pity.

455.   Dost thou hate the atheist because he does love not God? Then shouldst thou be disliked because thou dost not love God perfectly.

456.   There is one thing especially in which creeds and churches surrender themselves to the devil, and that is in their anathemas. When the priest chants Anathema Maranatha, then I see a devil worshipper praying.

457. No doubt, when the priest curses, he is crying to God; but it is the God of anger and darkness to whom he devotes himself along with his enemy; for as he approaches God, so shall God receive him.

458. I was much plagued by Satan, until I found that it was God who was tempting me; then the anguish of him passed out of my soul for ever.

459. I hated the devil and was sick with his temptations and tortures; and I could not tell why the voice in his departing words was so sweet that when he returned often and offered himself to me, it was with sorrow I refused him. Then I discovered it was Krishna at His tricks and my hate was changed into laughter.

460. They explained the evil in the world by saying that Satan had prevailed against God; but I think more proudly of my Beloved. I believe that nothing is done but by His will in heaven or hell, on earth or on the waters.

461. In our ignorance we are like children proud of our success in walking erect and unaided and too eager to be aware of the mother's steadying touch on the shoulder. When we wake, we look back and see that God was leading and upholding us always.

462. At first whenever I fell back into sin, I used to weep and rage against myself and against God for having suffered it. Afterwards it was as much as I could dare to ask, "Why hast thou rolled me again in the mud, O my playfellow?" Then even that came to my mind to seem too bold and

presumptuous; I could only get up in silence, look at him out of the corner of my eyes — and clean myself.

463.   God has so arranged life that the world is the soul's husband; Krishna its divine paramour. We owe a debt of service to the world and are bound to it by a law, a compelling opinion, and a common experience of pain and pleasure, but our heart's worship and our free and secret joy are for our Lover.

464.   The joy of God is secret and wonderful; it is a mystery and a rapture at which common sense makes mouths of mockery; but the soul that has once tasted it, can never renounce, whatever worldly disrepute, torture and affliction it may bring us.

465.   God, the world Guru, is wiser than thy mind; trust Him and not that eternal self-seeker & arrogant sceptic.

466.   The sceptic mind doubts always because it cannot understand, but the faith of the God-lover persists in knowing although it cannot understand. Both are necessary to our darkness, but there can be no doubt which is the mightier. What I cannot understand now, I shall some day master, but if I lose faith & love, I fall utterly from the goal which God has set before me.

467.   I may question God, my guide & teacher, & ask Him, "Am I right or hast Thou in thy love & wisdom suffered my mind to deceive me?" Doubt thy mind, if thou wilt, but doubt not that God leads thee.

468.   Because thou wert given at first imperfect conceptions about God, now thou ragest and deniest Him. Man, dost thou doubt thy teacher because he gave not thee the whole of knowledge at the beginning? Study rather that imperfect truth & put it in its place, so that thou mayst pass on safely to the wider knowledge that is now opening before thee.

469.   This is how God in His love teaches the child soul & the weakling, taking them step by step and withholding the vision of His ultimate & yet unattainable mountaintops. And have we not all some weakness? Are we not all in His sight but as little children?

470.   This I have seen that whatever God has withheld from me, He withheld in His love & wisdom. Had I grasped it then, I would have turned some great good into a great poison. Yet sometimes when we insist, He gives us poison to drink that we may learn to turn from it and taste with knowledge His ambrosia & His nectar.

471.   Even the atheist ought now to be able to see that creation marches towards some infinite & mighty purpose which evolution in its very nature supposes. But infinite purpose & fulfilment presupposes an infinite wisdom that prepares, guides, shapes, protects & justifies. Revere then that Wisdom & worship it with thoughts in thy soul if not with incense in a temple, and even though thou deny it the heart of infinite Love and the mind of infinite self-effulgence. Then though thou know it not it is still Krishna whom thou reverest & worshippest.

472.   The Lord of Love has said, "They who follow after

the Unknowable & Indefinable, follow after Me and I accept them." He has justified by His word the Illusionist & the Agnostic. Why then, O devotee, dost thou rail at him whom thy Master has accepted?

473.   Calvin who justified eternal Hell, knew not God but made one terrible mask of Him His eternal reality. If there were an unending Hell, it could only be a seat of unending rapture; for God is Ananda and than the eternity of His bliss there is no other eternity.

474.   Dante, when he said that God's perfect love created eternal Hell, wrote perhaps wiselier than he knew; for from stray glimpses I have sometimes thought there is a Hell where our souls suffer aeons of intolerable ecstasy & wallow as if for ever in the utter embrace of Rudra, the sweet & terrible.

475.   Discipleship to God the Teacher, sonship to God the Father, tenderness of God the Mother, clasp of the hand of the divine Friend, laughter and sport with our Comrade and boy Playfellow, blissful servitude to God the Master, rapturous love of our divine Paramour, these are the seven beatitudes of life in the human body. Canst thou unite all these in a single supreme & rainbow-hued relation? Then hast thou no need of any heaven and thou exceedest the emancipation of the Adwaitin.

476.   When will the world change into the model of heaven? When all mankind becomes boys & girls together with God revealed as Krishna & Kali, the happiest boy & strongest girl of the crowd, playing together in the gardens of Paradise. The Semitic Eden was well enough,

but Adam & Eve were too grown up and its God himself too old & stern & solemn for the offer of the Serpent to be resisted.

477.   The Semites have afflicted mankind with the conception of a God who is a stern & dignified king & solemn judge & knows not mirth. But we who have seen Krishna, know Him for a boy fond of play and a child full of mischief & happy laughter.

478.   A God who cannot smile, could not have created this humorous universe.

479.   God took a child to fondle him in His bosom of delight; but the mother wept & would not be consoled because her child no longer existed.

480.   When I suffer from pain or grief or mischance, I say "So, my old Playfellow, thou hast taken again to bullying me," and I sit down to possess the pleasure of the pain, the joy of the grief, the good fortune of the mischance; then He sees He is found out and takes His ghosts & bugbears away from me.

481.   The seeker after divine knowledge finds in the description of Krishna stealing the robes of the Gopis one of the deepest parables of God's ways with the soul, the devotee a perfect rendering in divine act of his heart's mystic experiences, the prurient & the Puritan (two faces of one temperament) only a lustful story. Men bring what they have in themselves and see it reflected in the Scripture.

482.   My lover took away my robe of sin and I let it fall,

rejoicing; then he plucked at my robe of virtue, but I was ashamed and alarmed and prevented him. It was not till he wrested it from me by force that I saw how my soul had been hidden from me.

483. Sin is a trick & a disguise of Krishna to conceal Himself from the gaze of the virtuous. Behold, O Pharisee, God in the sinner, sin in thy self purifying thy heart; clasp thy brother.

484. Love of God, charity towards men is the first step towards perfect wisdom.

485. He who condemns failure & imperfection, is condemning God; he limits his own soul and cheats his own vision. Condemn not, but observe Nature, help & heal thy brothers and strengthen by sympathy their capacities & their courage.

486. Love of man, love of woman, love of things, love of thy neighbour, love of thy country, love of animals, love of humanity are all the love of God reflected in these living images. So love & grow mighty to enjoy all, to help all and to love for ever.

487. If there are things that absolutely refuse to be transformed or remedied into God's more perfect image, they may be destroyed with tenderness in the heart, but ruthlessness in the smiting. But make sure first that God has given thee thy sword and thy mission.

488. I should love my neighbour not because he is neighbourhood, — for what is there in neighbourhood

and distance? nor because the religions tell me he is my brother, — for where is the root of that brotherhood? but because he is myself. Neighbourhood and distance affect the body, the heart goes beyond them. Brotherhood is of blood or country or religion or humanity, but when self-interest clamours what becomes of this brotherhood? It is only by living in God & turning mind and heart & body into the image of his universal unity that that deep, disinterested and unassailable love becomes possible.

489.   When I live in Krishna, then ego & self-interest vanish and only God himself can qualify my love bottomless & illimitable.

490.   Living in Krishna, even enmity becomes a play of love and the wrestling of brothers.

491.   To the soul that has hold of the highest beatitude, life cannot be an evil or a sorrowful illusion; rather all life becomes the rippling love and laughter of a divine Lover & Playfellow.

492.   Canst thou see God as the bodiless Infinite & yet love Him as a man loves his mistress? Then has the highest truth of the Infinite been revealed to thee. Canst thou also clothe the Infinite in one secret embraceable body and see Him seated in each & all of these bodies that are visible & sensible? Then has its widest & profoundest truth come also into thy possession.

493.   Divine Love has simultaneously a double play, an universal movement, deep, calm & bottomless like the

nether Ocean, which broods upon the whole world and each thing that is in it as upon a level bed with an equal pressure, and a personal movement, forceful, intense & ecstatic like the dancing surface of the same Ocean, which varies the height & force of its billows and chooses the objects it shall fall upon with the kiss of its foam & spray and the clasp of its engulfing waters.

494.   I used to hate and avoid pain and resent its infliction; but now I find that had I not so suffered, I would not now possess, trained and perfected, this infinitely & multitudinously sensible capacity of delight in my mind, heart and body. God justifies himself in the end even when He has masked Himself as a bully and a tyrant.

495.   I swore that I would not suffer from the world's grief and the world's stupidity and cruelty & injustice and I made my heart as hard in endurance as the nether millstone and my mind as a polished surface of steel. I no longer suffered, but enjoyment had passed away from me. Then God broke my heart and ploughed up my mind. I rose through cruel & incessant anguish to a blissful painlessness and through sorrow and indignation & revolt to an infinite knowledge and a settled peace.

496.   When I found that pain was the reverse side & the training of delight, I sought to heap blows on myself & multiply suffering in all my members; for even God's tortures seemed to me slow & slight & inefficient. Then my Lover had to stay my hand & cry, "Cease; for my stripes are enough for thee."

497.   The self-torture of the old monks & penitents was

perverse & stupid; yet was there a secret soul of knowledge behind their perversities.

498.   God is our wise & perfect Friend; because he knows when to smite as well as when to fondle, when to slay us no less than when to save & to succour.

499.   The divine Friend of all creatures conceals His friendliness in the mask of an enemy till He has made us ready for the highest heavens; then, as in Kurukshetra, the terrible form of the Master of strife, suffering & destruction is withdrawn & the sweet face, the tender arm, the oft-clasped body of Krishna shine out on the shaken soul & purified eyes of his eternal comrade & playmate.

500.   Suffering makes us capable of the full force of the Master of Delight; it makes us capable also to bear the utter play of the Master of Power. Pain is the key that opens the gates of strength; it is the high-road that leads to the city of beatitude.

501.   Yet, O soul of man, seek not after pain, for that is not His will, seek after His joy only; as for suffering, it will come to thee surely in His providence as often and as much as is needed for thee. Then bear it that thou mayst find out at last its heart of rapture.

502.   Neither do thou inflict pain, O man, on thy fellow; God alone has the right to inflict pain; or those have it whom He has commissioned. But deem not fanatically, as did Torquemada, that thou art one of these.

503. In former times there was a noble form of asseveration for souls compact merely of force and action, "As surely as God liveth." But for our modern needs another asseveration would suit better, "As surely as God loveth."

504. Science is chiefly useful to the God-lover & the God-knower because it enables him to understand in detail and admire the curious wonders of His material workmanship. The one learns & cries, "Behold how the Spirit has manifested itself in matter"; the other, "Behold, the touch of my Lover & Master, the perfect Artist, the hand omnipotent."

505. O Aristophanes of the universe, thou who watchest thy world and laughest sweetly to thyself, wilt thou not let me too see with divine eyes and share in thy worldwide laughters?

506. Kalidasa says in a daring image that the snow-rocks of Kailasa are Shiva's loud world-laughters piled up in utter whiteness & pureness on the mountaintops. It is true; and when their image falls on the heart, then the world's cares melt away like the clouds below into their real nothingness.

507. The strangest of the soul's experiences is this, that it finds, when it ceases to care for the image & threat of troubles, then the troubles themselves are nowhere to be found in one's neighbourhood. It is then that we hear from behind those unreal clouds God laughing at us.

508. Has thy effort succeeded, O thou Titan? Dost thou sit, like Ravana and Hiranyakashipou, served by the gods and the world's master? But that which thy soul was really hunting after, has escaped from thee.

509. Ravana's mind thought it was hungering after universal sovereignty and victory over Rama; but the aim his soul kept its vision fixed upon all the time was to get back to its heaven as soon as possible & be again God's menial. Therefore, as the shortest way, it hurled itself against God in a furious clasp of enmity.

510. The greatest of joys is to be, like Naraka, the slave of God; the worst of Hells, being abandoned of God, to be the world's master. That which seems nearest to the ignorant conception of God, is the farthest from him.

511. God's servant is something; God's slave is greater.

512. To be master of the world would indeed be supreme felicity, if one were universally loved; but for that one would have to be at the same time the slave of all humanity.

513. After all when thou countest up thy long service to God, thou wilt find thy supreme work was the flawed & little good thou didst in love for humanity.

514. There are two works that are perfectly pleasing to God in his servant; to sweep in silent adoration His temple-floors and to fight in the world's battlefield for His divine consummation in humanity.

515. He who has done even a little good to human beings, though he be the worst of sinners, is accepted by God in the ranks of His lovers and servants. He shall look upon the face of the Eternal.

516. O fool of thy weakness, cover not God's face from

thyself by a veil of awe, approach Him not with a suppliant weakness. Look! thou wilt see on His face not the solemnity of the King & Judge, but the smile of the Lover.

517.   Until thou canst learn to grapple with God as a wrestler with his comrade, thy soul's strength shall always be hid from thee.

518.   Sumbha first loved Kali with his heart & body, then was furious with her and fought her, at last prevailed against her, seized her by the hair & whirled her thrice round him in the heavens; the next moment he was slain by her. These are the Titan's four strides to immortality and of them all the last is the longest and mightiest.

519.   Kali is Krishna revealed as dreadful Power & wrathful Love. She slays with her furious blows the self in body, life & mind in order to liberate it as spirit eternal.

520.   Our parents fell, in the deep Semitic apologue, because they tasted the fruit of the tree of good and evil. Had they taken at once of the tree of eternal life, they would have escaped the immediate consequence; but God's purpose in humanity would have been defeated. His wrath is our eternal advantage.

521.   If Hell were possible, it would be the shortest cut to the highest heaven. For verily God loveth.

522.   God drives us out [of] every Eden that we may be forced to travel through the desert to a diviner Paradise. If thou wonder why should that parched & fierce transit

be necessary, then art thou befooled by thy mind and hast not studied thy soul behind and its dim desires and secret raptures.

523.   A healthy mind hates pain; for the desire of pain that men sometimes develop in their minds is morbid and contrary to Nature. But the soul cares not for the mind & its sufferings any more than the iron-master for the pain of the ore in the furnace; it follows its own necessities and its own hunger.

524.   Pity is sometimes a good substitute for love; but it is always no more than a substitute.

525.   Self-pity is always born of self-love; but pity for others is not always born of love for its object. It is sometimes a self-regarding shrinking from the sight of pain; sometimes the rich man's contemptuous dole to the pauper. Develop rather God's divine compassion than human pity.

526.   Not pity that bites the heart and weakens the inner members, but a divine masterful & untroubled compassion and helpfulness is the virtue that we should encourage.

527.   To find that saving a man's body or mind from suffering is not always for the good of either soul, mind or body, is one of the bitterest of experiences for the humanly compassionate.

528.   Human pity is born of ignorance & weakness; it is the slave of emotional impressions. Divine compassion understands, discerns & saves.

529.   Indiscriminate compassion is the noblest gift of temperament, not to do even the least hurt to one living thing is the highest of all human virtues; but God practises neither. Is man therefore nobler and better than the All-loving?

530.   Love and serve men, but beware lest thou desire their approbation. Obey rather God within thee.

531.   Not to have heard the voice of God and His angels is the world's idea of sanity.

532.   See God everywhere and be not frightened by masks. Believe that all falsehood is truth in the making or truth in the breaking, all failure an effectuality concealed, all weakness strength hiding itself from its own vision, all pain a secret & violent ecstasy. If thou believest firmly & unweariedly, in the end thou wilt see & experience the All-true, Almighty & All-blissful.

533.   Human love fails by its own ecstasy, human strength is exhausted by its own effort, human knowledge throws a shadow that conceals half the globe of truth from its own sunlight; but divine knowledge embraces opposite truths & reconciles them, divine strength grows by the prodigality of its self-expenditure, divine love can squander itself utterly, yet never waste or diminish.

534.   The rejection of falsehood by the mind seeking after truth is one of the chief causes why mind cannot attain to the settled, rounded & perfect truth; not to escape falsehood is the effort of divine mind, but to seize the truth which lies masked behind even the most grotesque or far-wandering error.

535.   The whole truth about any object is a rounded & all-embracing globe which for ever circles around, but never touches the one & only subject & object of knowledge, God.

536.   There are many profound truths which are like weapons dangerous to the unpractised wielder. Rightly handled, they are the most precious & potent in God's armoury.

537.   The obstinate pertinacity with which we cling to our meagre, fragmentary, night-besieged & grief-besieged individual existence even while the unbroken bliss of our universal life calls to us, is one of the most amazing of God's mysteries. It is only equalled by the infinite blindness with which we cast a shadow of our ego over the whole world & call that the universal being. These two darknesses are the very essence & potency of Maya.

538.   Atheism is the shadow or dark side of the highest perception of God. Every formula we frame about God, though always true as a symbol, becomes false when we accept it as a sufficient formula. The Atheist & Agnostic come to remind us of our error.

539.   God's negations are as useful to us as His affirmations. It is He who as the Atheist denies His own existence for the better perfecting of human knowledge. It is not enough to see God in Christ & Ramakrishna & hear His words, we must see Him and hear Him also in Huxley & Haeckel.

540.   Canst thou see God in thy torturer & slayer even in

thy moment of death or thy hours of torture? Canst thou see Him in that which thou art slaying, see & love even while thou slayest? Thou hast thy hand on the supreme knowledge. How shall he attain to Krishna who has never worshipped Kali?

Additional Aphorisms

541.   I know that the opposite of what I say is true, but for the present what I say is still truer.

542.   I believe with you, my friends, that God, if He exists, is a demon and an ogre. But after all what are you going to do about it?

*

543.   God is the supreme Jesuit Father. He is ever doing evil that good may come of it; ever misleads for a greater leading; ever oppresses our will that it may arrive at last at an infinite freedom.

544.   Our Evil is to God not evil, but ignorance and imperfection, our good a lesser imperfection.

545.   The religionist speaks a truth, though too violently, when he tells us that even our greatest and purest virtue is as vileness before the divine nature of God.

546.   To be beyond good and evil is not to act sin or virtue indifferently, but to arrive at a high and universal good.

547.   That good is not our ethical virtue which is a relative and erring light in the world; it is supra-ethical and divine.

Note on the Texts

In or around 1913, Sri Aurobindo wrote 552 aphorisms in a single notebook. In May 1915 and May 1916 he published ten of them in the monthly review *Arya*. (These ten have not been reproduced here. They form part of *Thoughts and Glimpses*, included in *Essays in Philosophy and Yoga*, volume 13 of The Complete Works of Sri Aurobindo.) Of the remaining 542 aphorisms, two are classed with the "Additional Aphorisms" (see below). This leaves 540 aphorisms forming the main series of *Thoughts and Aphorisms*.

In the notebook, the aphorisms were written in nine groupings, three of which are headed Jnana, three Karma and three Bhakti. The groupings occur in this order: Jnana, Karma, Bhakti, Karma, Jnana, Bhakti, Karma, Bhakti, Jnana. The editors have placed the three groupings of Jnana, the three groupings of Karma and the three groupings of Bhakti together. Sri Aurobindo numbered all the aphorisms in Jnana and Karma, none of those in Bhakti. Since it appears that he intended the numbers to form part of the text, the editors have placed a number before each aphorism. These numbers do not correspond to those in the manuscript because the three groupings of each section have been placed together and the unnumbered Bhakti section included.

Sri Aurobindo left indications in the manuscript that certain aphorisms were to be moved to a different part or position. For example, he seems to have wanted present aphorisms 240 and 241 to be placed after present aphorism

98. But since some of these manuscript indications are not clear, the editors have followed the original notebook order.

The manuscript, entirely handwritten, was revised once or twice by Sri Aurobindo. The original writing is mostly clear, but the revision is sometimes cramped and difficult to read. The words "shape" in aphorism 19 and "self-unity" in aphorism 205 are doubtful readings.

The last two aphorisms (541–42) in the notebook containing the main series do not seem to have been intended for inclusion in the Karma, Jnana or Bhakti sections. The editors have placed them in a separate section headed "Additional Aphorisms" along with five other aphorisms (543–47) that were written in a different notebook. The handwriting of these last five indicates that they were written somewhat later than 1913 — possibly as late as 1919.

Thoughts and Aphorisms was first published in 1958. A second impression of the first edition was issued in 1959. New editions, textually identical to the first, came out in 1968 and 1971. The editions of 1977 and 1982 contained some corrections of transcription errors. The text of the present, sixth edition is identical to the one published in *Essays Divine and Human*, Volume 12 of The Complte Works of Sri Aurobindo.